MONROEVILLE PUBLIC LIBRARY

3 3081 10130356 9

W9-BME-438

Word Bird's

Hats

ε

Published in the United States of America by The Child's World®, Inc.
PO Box 326
Chanhassen, MN 55317-0326
800-599-READ
www.childsworld.com

Project Manager Mary Berendes
Editor Katherine Stevenson, Ph.D.
Designer Ian Butterworth

Copyright © 2003 by The Child's World®, Inc.
All rights reserved. No part of this book may be
reproduced or utilized in any form or by any means
without written permission from the publisher.

Library of Congress Cataloging-in-Publication Data
Moncure, Jane Belk.
Word Bird's hats / by Jane Belk Moncure.
p. cm.
Summary: Over the course of a week, Word Bird tries on hats
representing different occupations and assembles the tools
he would need for each job.
ISBN 1-56766-997-2 (lib. : alk. paper)
[1. Occupations—Fiction. 2. Hats—Fiction. 3. Birds—Fiction.]
I. Title.
PZ7.M739 Wp 2002
[E]—dc21
2001006043

Word  Bird's™

Hats

by Jane Belk Moncure
illustrated by Chris McEwan

PUBLIC LIBRARY

√ JAN 1 4 2003

MONROEVILLE, PA

On Sunday,
Word Bird put on a

cook's hat.

"Today I will be a cook,"
Word Bird said. "I will
fix breakfast."

What did Word Bird need?

A kitchen,

pots,

pans,

a mixer,

spoons.

What else?

On Monday, Word Bird put on a

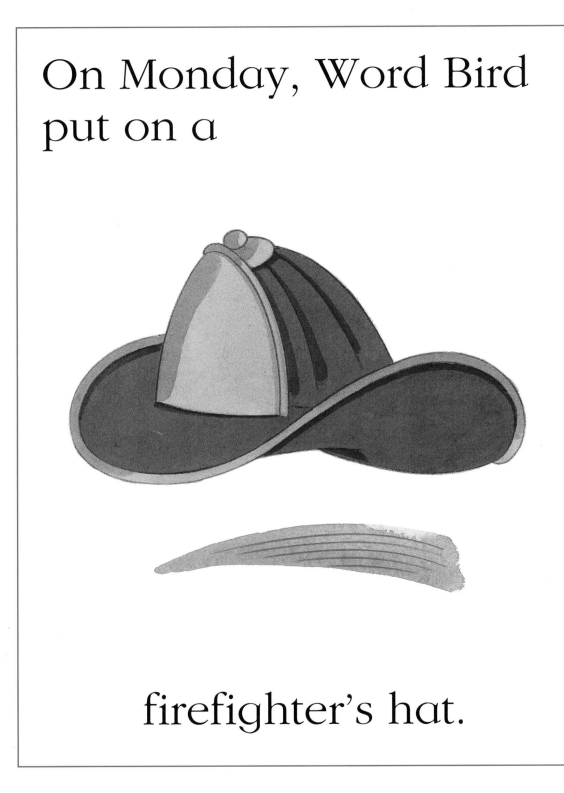

firefighter's hat.

"Today I will be a
firefighter," Word
Bird said.

What did Word Bird need?

A fire truck,

a ladder,

a hose,

a fire bell.

What else?

On Tuesday,
Word Bird put on a

cowboy hat.

"Today I will be a cowboy,"
Word Bird said.

What did Word Bird need?

A horse,

a rope,

a saddle,

a cow.

What else?

On Wednesday,
Word Bird put on a

pilot's hat.

"Today I will be a pilot,"
Word Bird said.

What did Word Bird need?

An airplane,

a parachute,

an airport.

What else?

On Thursday,
Word Bird put on a

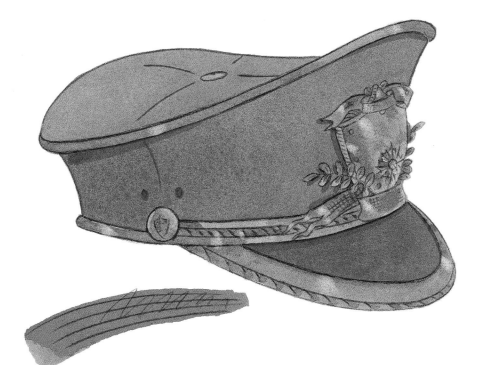

police officer's hat.

"Today I will be a police officer," Word Bird said.

What did Word Bird need?

A police car,

a whistle,

a police badge,

a police dog,

a two-way
radio.

What else?

On Friday,
Word Bird put on a

mail carrier's hat.

"Today I will be a mail carrier," Word Bird said.

What did Word Bird need?

A mail truck,

letters,

packages,

a mailbox.

What else?

On Saturday,
Word Bird put on a

farmer's hat.

"Today I will be a farmer,"
Word Bird said. "I will
plant seeds."

What did Word Bird need?

A tractor,

a rake,

a hoe,

seeds,

water.

What else?

Can you read these words with Word Bird?

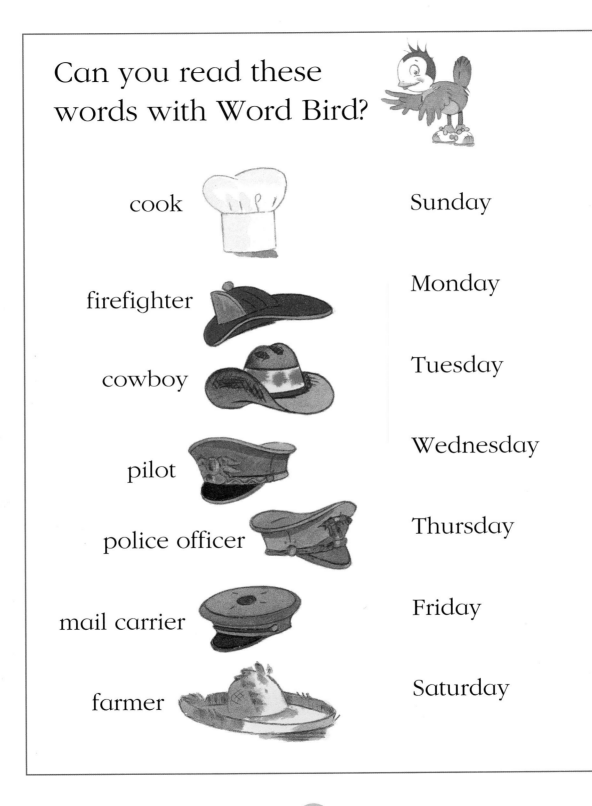

cook

firefighter

cowboy

pilot

police officer

mail carrier

farmer

Sunday

Monday

Tuesday

Wednesday

Thursday

Friday

Saturday